# The Effects of Military Base Closures on Local Communities

*A Short-Term Perspective*

Michael Dardia
Kevin F. McCarthy
Jesse Malkin
Georges Vernez

National Defense Research Institute

*Prepared for the
Office of the Secretary of Defense*

**RAND**

Approved for public release; distribution unlimited

UA
23.3
.E4
1996

| DATE DUE | | | |
|---|---|---|---|
| | | | |
| | | | |
| | | | |
| | | | |
| | | | |
| | | | |
| | | | |
| | | | |
| | | | |
| | | | |
| | | | |

This book may be RECALLED before its due date

GAYLORD  PRINTED IN U.S.A.

APR 25 1996

# PREFACE

This report is one of a series written as part of a project that investigates the effects of the defense draw-down on California's economy. This report investigates the effects of declining defense outlays on small suppliers to aerospace manufacturers. Others in the series examine the effects of military base closures in the state's communities and the effect of declining defense budgets on workers in the aerospace industry.

The project was sponsored by the Office of the Undersecretary of Defense (Personnel and Readiness). It was carried out in the Forces and Resources Policy Center of the National Defense Research Institute, a federally funded research and development center sponsored by the Office of the Secretary of Defense, the Joint Staff, and the defense agencies.

This report and its companion pieces (listed below) should interest anyone involved in the interactions between the Department of Defense, its contractors and suppliers, and civilian communities.

> Georges Vernez, Michael Dardia, Kevin F. McCarthy, Jesse Malkin, and Robert Nordyke, *California's Shrinking Defense Contractors: Effects on Small Suppliers*, Santa Monica, Calif.: RAND, MR-687-OSD, 1996.

> Robert F. Schoeni, Michael Dardia, Kevin F. McCarthy, and Georges Vernez, *Life After Cutbacks: Tracking California's Aerospace Workers*, Santa Monica, Calif.: RAND, MR-688-OSD, 1996.

# CONTENTS

Preface . . . . . . . . . . . . . . . . . . . . . . . . . . . . . . . . . . . . . . . . . iii

Figures . . . . . . . . . . . . . . . . . . . . . . . . . . . . . . . . . . . . . . . . . vii

Tables . . . . . . . . . . . . . . . . . . . . . . . . . . . . . . . . . . . . . . . . . . ix

Summary . . . . . . . . . . . . . . . . . . . . . . . . . . . . . . . . . . . . . . . . xi

Chapter One
  INTRODUCTION . . . . . . . . . . . . . . . . . . . . . . . . . . . . . 1
  Background . . . . . . . . . . . . . . . . . . . . . . . . . . . . . . . . . 1
  Purpose of This Study . . . . . . . . . . . . . . . . . . . . . . . . . . 3
  How This Document Is Organized . . . . . . . . . . . . . . . . . . 5

Chapter Two
  OUTLINE OF THE STUDY . . . . . . . . . . . . . . . . . . . . . . . 7
  Prior Studies . . . . . . . . . . . . . . . . . . . . . . . . . . . . . . . . 7
  Base Characteristics . . . . . . . . . . . . . . . . . . . . . . . . . . . 10
  Community Characteristics . . . . . . . . . . . . . . . . . . . . . . 12

Chapter Three
  STUDY PLAN . . . . . . . . . . . . . . . . . . . . . . . . . . . . . . . . 15
  Case Selection . . . . . . . . . . . . . . . . . . . . . . . . . . . . . . . 16
  Profile of Bases Selected . . . . . . . . . . . . . . . . . . . . . . . . 16
    George Air Force Base . . . . . . . . . . . . . . . . . . . . . . . . 16
    Fort Ord . . . . . . . . . . . . . . . . . . . . . . . . . . . . . . . . . . 18
    Castle Air Force Base . . . . . . . . . . . . . . . . . . . . . . . . . 19
  Analytical Approach . . . . . . . . . . . . . . . . . . . . . . . . . . . 20
    Evaluation Measures . . . . . . . . . . . . . . . . . . . . . . . . . 20
    Benchmarks for Comparisons . . . . . . . . . . . . . . . . . . . 22

Chapter Four
  ANALYSIS ................................... 25
  Basic Description ............................ 25
  Comparison with Projections .................... 31
  Comparison with Matched Bases ................. 34
  Comparison with County Totals .................. 38

Chapter Five
  RESULTS AND CONCLUSIONS ................... 43
  Results ..................................... 43
  Conclusions ................................. 44

Appendix
A.  SOURCES OF FORECASTS ...................... 47
B.  DATA SOURCES .............................. 49
C.  LOCAL IMPACT AREAS ........................ 55

References ...................................... 57

# FIGURES

| | | |
|---|---|---|
| 2.1. | Conceptual Model of Effects of Base and Community Characteristics | 10 |
| 3.1. | Base Employment, 1989–1994 | 17 |
| 3.2. | Location of Bases Selected for Study | 18 |
| 4.1. | Population Trends, 1981–1994 | 25 |
| 4.2. | Community Changes Since Base Closure | 27 |
| 4.3. | Housing Prices Around George AFB | 28 |
| 4.4. | Housing Prices Around Castle AFB | 28 |
| 4.5. | Housing Prices Around Fort Ord | 29 |
| 4.6. | Projected Versus Actual Changes, George AFB | 32 |
| 4.7. | Projected Versus Actual Changes, Castle AFB | 32 |
| 4.8. | Projected Versus Actual Changes, Fort Ord | 33 |
| 4.9. | George AFB Versus Vandenberg AFB, 1989–1994 Changes | 37 |
| 4.10. | Castle AFB Versus Beale AFB, 1991–1994 Changes | 37 |
| 4.11. | Fort Ord Versus Camp Pendleton, 1991–1994 Changes | 38 |
| 4.12. | George AFB Versus San Bernardino County, 1989–1994 | 39 |
| 4.13. | Castle AFB Versus Merced County, 1991–1994 | 40 |
| 4.14. | Fort Ord Versus Monterey County, 1991–1994 | 41 |

# TABLES

1.1. Major California Bases Slated for Closure . . . . . . . . . .   3
2.1. Active Duty and Retiree Populations in Base Communities . . . . . . . . . . . . . . . . . . . . . . . . . . . . .  13
3.1. Measures . . . . . . . . . . . . . . . . . . . . . . . . . . . . . . . .  21
C.1. Local Impact Area Cities and Their Zip Codes . . . . . .  56

# SUMMARY

## THE PROBLEM

Amid the decline in defense spending following the end of the Cold War, military base closures have prompted some of the most vocal public concerns. Public expectations of the impact often verge on the apocalyptic, and economic forecasts of the local effects seem to bolster such fears. While many studies have been done on the closure and revitalization process, little new work has been done on the immediate economic impacts of base closures since the wave of closures after the Vietnam War. This study examined the experience of the communities surrounding three of the largest bases closed in California since 1988. The bases were selected due to their large presence in the local community and to the fact that the communities were sufficiently isolated geographically that the effects could be expected to be both severe and measurable.

## HOW WE STUDIED THE PROBLEM

The study used a case-study approach to examine the impact on nearby communities of three base closures:

- George Air Force Base (AFB), located in San Bernardino County, which closed in December 1992

- Fort Ord, located in Monterey County, which closed in September 1994

- Castle Air Force Base, located in Merced County, which was slated for closure in 1995 and from which 65 percent of its uniformed personnel had been vacated by October 1994.

To assess the impact of base closures on local communities, the study used nine measures—two centering on changes in population, four on changes in employment, and three on changes in the housing market. The study investigated how the closures impacted the size of the total population in nearby communities and the size of those communities' school enrollments. It looked at the size of neighboring communities' labor forces, their unemployment rates, their taxable retail sales, and their municipal revenues. It also explored the number of housing units in adjacent communities, their vacancy rates, and the average sale prices of owner-occupied housing. For each community, the study analyzed how each measure behaved before and after the closure of the selected bases.

The study compared these findings against three benchmarks: (1) the changes that various expert consultant studies had predicted would occur in each community, (2) the experience of a matched set of California bases that had not been scheduled for closure, and (3) the experience of other communities in each affected county.

## WHAT WE FOUND OUT ABOUT IT

While some of the communities did indeed suffer, the effects were

- not catastrophic
- not nearly as severe as forecasted.

This finding does not deny the very real costs of job loss borne by displaced workers and their families or the revenue losses suffered by local businesses. These effects underscore the point that, as is the case with defense industry cutbacks (Dertouzos and Dardia, 1993), the burden of defense cuts falls on the individual worker or firm rather than the community.

In addition to comparing the communities' actual and forecasted experiences, we also examined the experience of the counties in which they are located and that of communities surrounding a set of matched bases that remained open. Though the closures had noticeable effects, they are relatively localized and have been at least partly offset by other economic factors.

Generalizing from the experiences of three bases is problematic, but the results suggest that the effects of base closure on local communities are not nearly as straightforward as some might believe. The degree of integration between bases and local communities and the characteristics of base personnel and local communities can interact to compound or moderate the effects that base closings will have on local communities. As a result, these findings highlight the importance of measuring changes in local communities as they occur to determine the actual effects of base closures. The alternatives are to rely either on long-term studies of the closure process, which lack the timeliness needed for effective mitigation, or on prior projections of the effects of closure, which sometimes lack credibility and are conducted before closure occurs in any case. Although there are many data problems that on-going monitoring must confront, this study demonstrates that such problems can be overcome. Indeed, one of the major contributions of this study is that it provides a model to use for such monitoring efforts.

Chapter One
# INTRODUCTION

## BACKGROUND

One of the most politically contentious adjustments to the decline in defense spending after the end of the Cold War has been the subject of military base closures. While the decline in military force structure and in weapons procurement has largely been a matter for the Department of Defense to decide, the question of which military bases to close was deemed too sensitive to be left to normal decision channels. (See, for example, Schmitt, 1993.) Instead, the Base Realignment and Adjustment Commission (BRAC) was established in order to shield the process from political influences.

Much of this sensitivity is due to concern for the fate of the communities surrounding the closed bases; such concerns are understandable in light of the fact that in many of these communities the base personnel—both military and civilian—represent a significant share of local employment and population. Even communities with promising alternative uses for the local base seem wary of the immediate effects of the closure, with its loss of civilian jobs and service members' local purchases. While the long-run experience with closed bases seems benign (Office of Economic Adjustment, 1993), little is known about the size or distribution of the more immediate impacts of base closures.[1] If the effects are adverse, they should be

---

[1] The 1985 OEA report looked at bases closed in the 1960s and 1970s and compared employment levels on the base and in neighboring communities at their peak and 10 to 15 years later. It found that employment levels from the new activities on the bases

most severe immediately after the closure, before there is time for labor markets to clear and for the compensatory effects of base reuse to come into play.

Since the recent wave of base closures began in 1989, 163 bases with 119,000 military and civilian personnel have been marked for closure.[2] Through the 1993 round of closures, California has absorbed a disproportionate share of the closed bases and displaced personnel, losing 82,000 military and civilian personnel on 21 bases. This is in sharp contrast to the previous wave of base closures after the Vietnam War, when the state lost only 7 out of the 100 bases closed nationally, totaling less than 5 percent of the national personnel declines. Table 1.1 lists the largest bases slated for closure in California for each of the last three rounds along with the number of affected personnel. (Several additional bases at which alignments—some major—were ordered are not listed.) These losses come at the same time that weapons procurement cutbacks have cost the state more than 300,000 jobs in the private sector, deepening and lengthening the recent recession.

These facts have led to a series of dire predictions about the cumulative impact of these losses on the state and its prospects for future growth, and much concern and preparation for the 1995 round of closures.[3] For example, the California Military Base Reuse Task Force (1994) projected that the unemployment rate in Merced County would jump to 21.7 percent from 14.4 percent, and that Monterey County's unemployment rate would rise to 18.5 percent from 10.3 percent, solely as a result of base closures.

---

(schools, industrial parks, airports, etc.) were generally larger than the original base employment.

[2]There are various estimates of the actual number of personnel at any given base. Unless otherwise noted, we have used estimates from each base or its Impact Analyses. See Appendix B for detailed descriptions of the data sources used in the study.

[3]This year's round was originally rumored to be as severe as the last three rounds combined, but in fact, was a little smaller than the size of the average of the last three cuts. Indeed, about 20,000 military and civilian jobs were cut in the latest round (three bases closed and two realigned) compared with an average of 27,000 in the three previous BRAC rounds. Two years ago, former Defense Secretary Aspin predicted that the 1995 round would be "the mother of all base closings" (see Pine, 1995). More recent reports seem to indicate that this round's closure will not be as ambitious as originally billed (Ricks, 1995).

## Table 1.1

### Major California Bases Slated for Closure

| Base | BRAC Round | Closure Date | Military Personnel | Civilian Workers |
|---|---|---|---|---|
| George AFB | 1988 | 1992 | 4,852 | 506 |
| Norton AFB | 1988 | 1994 | 4,520 | 2,133 |
| Presidio | 1988 | 1995 | 2,140 | 3,150 |
| Castle AFB | 1991 | 1995 | 5,239 | 1,164 |
| Fort Ord | 1991 | 1994 | 13,619 | 2,835 |
| Long Beach Naval Station | 1991 | 1994 | 9,519 | 833 |
| Marine Corps Air Station | 1993 | 1999 | 5,689 | 979 |
| Mare Island Naval Shipyard | 1993 | 1996 | 7,567 | 1,963 |
| Alameda Naval Air Station | 1993 | 1997 | 10,586 | 556 |
| Naval Training Center (San Diego) | 1993 | 1998 | 5,186 | 40 |

SOURCE: Innes et al. (1994). Only bases with greater than 5,000 total personnel are listed.

## PURPOSE OF THIS STUDY

The political uproar surrounding these projections poses an important issue for policymakers: Should they provide special assistance to local communities to aid them in adjusting to base closures? This issue, in turn, raises two related problems: How do policymakers determine the effects of closures on the surrounding communities in a timely fashion and what standard do they apply to determine if special assistance is warranted?

As described in the next section, generally two classes of studies have been done on base closure. The first are estimates of the anticipated effects conducted before the closures actually occur. Such studies are often commissioned by the communities that will be directly affected by the closure. The second are studies looking at the long-term effects of closure. Such studies are typically conducted several years after the closure has occurred.

Both studies pose problems for policymakers. Those in the first class are often problematic given their political motivation[4] and the fact

---

[4]Such studies are often, but not always, conducted to lobby against proposed base closures.

that they represent forecasts, not actual outcomes. Studies of the second sort, on the other hand, are likely to be available too late to permit a timely policy response. Indeed, both types must deal with the absence of systematic and timely data available below the county level. The current study attempts to fill this gap by measuring the effects of base closure along a variety of dimensions that group into three general categories: declines in population, employment, and housing demand.

The second problem policymakers face is the choice of standard to use in assessing the actual changes that have occurred. From a policy perspective, the issue here is not simply whether a community suffered some adverse effects from base closure but, rather, how serious and long-lasting those negative effects are likely to be. In particular, policymakers are concerned that no one community bears a disproportionate share of the costs of defense downsizing. Indeed, one could argue that just as communities with bases may have benefited from the bases' presence in the past, they can be expected to bear part of the costs of the base closure process. They should not, however, have to bear costs that are widely out of proportion to past or future benefits. Although clear in principle, this standard is not readily translated into a specific measure. Correspondingly, this analysis uses several different benchmarks to assess the degree of change that has occurred in the local communities.

In combination, this analysis highlights the importance of measuring the short-term effects of base closure (instead of simply relying on community-level forecasts) as well as how difficult this measurement can be. Nonetheless, a word of caution about this analysis is warranted. Due to data constraints and the small number of bases examined, rigorous analysis of the impacts of the recent waves of base closures on communities is not attempted here. Thus, despite our use of multiple measures of the effects of closure and multiple standards of comparison, data limitations prevent us from generalizing from these results to other bases that might be closed in the future. Nonetheless, the results of this analysis do agree with the findings of earlier studies as to the highly localized effects of closure. The recency of these closures, however, prevents us from determining how short-lived these effects may be.

## HOW THIS DOCUMENT IS ORGANIZED

The next chapter describes the characteristics of the bases and communities studied, and Chapter Three outlines the study design, including how the bases were selected, their profiles, and the analytic plan of the study. Chapter Four presents the results of the analysis and compares them with the benchmark bases and communities. The final Chapter contains the study findings and conclusions. The document also has three appendices. These contain the sources of the forecasts of the economic effect of the base closings, the sources of our data, and a description of how we defined the local impact areas.

# Chapter Two
# OUTLINE OF THE STUDY

Bases lie on a continuum from the highly self-contained military training bases with a preponderance of uniformed personnel to the largely civilian-manned depots and shipyards that approach the defense industry in their connection to the local economy. The surrounding communities range from small isolated communities with little developed industry to major metropolitan areas with highly diversified economies.

In addition to these static qualities of bases and communities, the impact of any economic shock such as a base closure depends on the underlying strength of the local economy as well as the business cycle at the time of the closure. This section describes some of the characteristics of military bases that can influence the economic effect of closures on local communities. It also discusses the characteristics of the community that can dampen or enhance the effect of base closures.

## PRIOR STUDIES

Despite concerns about the effects of base closure, policymakers have little information to guide their assessments of which communities might need special assistance and the types of assistance to provide. Two types of information are available on the effects of base closure on local communities: (1) studies of the long-term impact of earlier rounds of closures and (2) projections of the effects of the recent round of closures. Each tends to produce a somewhat different picture of base closure effects.

Studies of earlier base closures are generally optimistic about communities' ability to recover.[1] For example, Daicoff et al. (1970) found little effect when the employment loss is less than 5 percent of total area employment. Both they and MacKinnon (1978) found no net loss in employment, although there may be some loss of high-wage jobs. Both studies emphasize that the major effect is felt in housing markets (through loss of equity and reductions in new construction). The most extensive study of the long-term effects of base closures (DoD, 1994), found that over the longer term, employment tends to surpass preclosure levels.

Jointly these studies call attention to several factors that should be kept in mind when considering the effects of base closures on local communities. First, the overall level of economic growth in the area (as well as the nation) will condition the effects of base closure. Second, the transfer of civilian personnel and the employed spouses of military personnel can create substantial job openings for local residents. Third, many of the bases are not closely integrated into their local communities; thus, the loss of base personnel does not necessarily translate into sharp reductions in retail sales to local business. Finally, reuse of bases provides communities with new economic opportunities that can become sources of employment and earnings. In sum, these studies suggest that over the longer term, communities tend to recover and often improve on their preclosure economies.

Projections of the effects of the recent round of closures tend to be more pessimistic—often warning of the severe and wide-ranging nature of the anticipated effects. To some extent, this gloomy tone can be attributed to the fact that such studies are often commissioned by local governments that are trying to lobby against closure. But that is not the only factor. Indeed, two central questions for such studies are what economic multiplier[2] to use and what base to apply it to. Innes et al. (1994) report that the least professional studies of-

---

[1] These studies are reviewed in Innes et al. (1994).

[2] The economic multiplier measures the effect that an increase (or decrease) in a specific eonomic activity has on the economy at large through its effects on demand for supplies and/or through its effect on incomes.

ten use very high multipliers,[3] but they also note that the appropriate multiplier may well vary with the size of the community in which the base is located. Because local suppliers provide very little in the way of goods and services to bases in small communities, the appropriate multiplier in these communities is likely to be smaller than in larger areas. Similar questions arise as to how to calculate the loss of direct spending in the local community as a result of the base closure. Spending effects, for example, are likely to vary depending upon whether personnel live on or off base, whether the jobs lost are military or civilian, how many spouses are employed in the community, etc. In other words, even those estimates that don't operate with a foregone conclusion still face difficult decisions as to how to estimate base closure effects.

These difficulties reflect the variety of outcomes that can follow base closure: residents who worked on the base and have lost their jobs can either look for jobs in the local labor market or leave the community to work elsewhere; local businesses (including rental property owners) may lose the portion of their revenues that came from now-unemployed workers or from relocated base personnel or base purchases, but some local business (notably in health services) may gain revenues from retiree demand redirected from base facilities; and vacancies that are created in jobs formerly held by military dependents who have relocated may create new job opportunities for remaining local residents. Thus, while many effects of base closure can serve to reduce local labor and service sector demand, there are other forces acting to increase demand.

The next two sections discuss the characteristics of bases and communities that determine the impact of closure on the local economy. Although this study does not use a formal economic model to estimate the effects of base closure, Figure 2.1 summarizes the relevant factors considered, along with their hypothesized effects (+ or –). A plus sign (+) indicates that the larger the value, the better the outcome for the community; a minus sign (–) indicates the reverse.

---

[3]While Innes et al. believe appropriate multipliers lie in the range of 1.2 to 1.4, some studies have used multipliers of over 3.

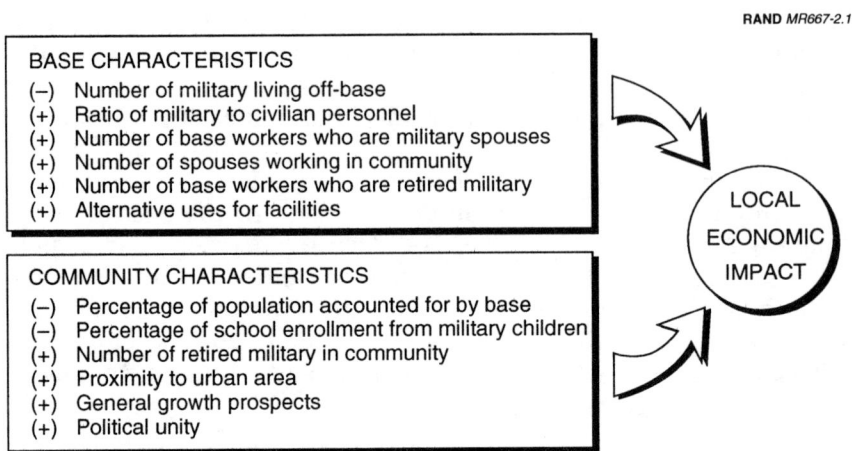

Figure 2.1—Conceptual Model of Effects of Base and Community Characteristics

## BASE CHARACTERISTICS

A number of factors attenuate the economic impact of base personnel on the local community. First, military personnel living on the base do not depend upon the local housing and retail service markets for their housing or their meals; thus, the more military personnel living on-post, the smaller the impact each service member has on the local community. In addition, military personnel—along with those civilian employees who are reservists or retired military—make a significant share of their retail purchases from the PX and other on-post businesses and do some or all of their banking at the base's credit union. This distinguishes them from civilian base workers who spend most of their disposable income in the community rather than on the base. The base also commonly supplies some school and hospital services for base personnel and their families, further attenuating their impact on the local community compared to civilian workers and the rest of the population. Last, because military personnel generally transfer to other bases when a base is closed, they leave the affected community and do not create demand for social services as might displaced civilian workers (and displaced defense industry workers).

Among military personnel, a sizable fraction have working spouses.[4] These spouses dilute the impact of base personnel whether they work on the base or in the community. If military spouses are civilian base workers, their discretionary spending is partly contained on the base, as is the case with military personnel, and they reduce the number of displaced civilian workers seeking jobs and requiring social services after the base closes. If, instead, the spouses work in the community—anecdotally in professional jobs such as teaching and nursing—their departure after base closure creates job openings in the community. While skill mismatches between the resident displaced civilian workers and the spouses' vacated jobs may occur (see Bradshaw, 1993), these vacancies still moderate the effect of closure on the local labor market; the more military spouses who work in the community or on the base, the better the outcome for the local community.

Some of the nonspouse civilian workers are retired military personnel and as noted above are eligible for many of the same base privileges as active duty personnel. After base closure, these workers (and their dependents) are apt to redirect their discretionary spending and demand for medical services to the local community. These workers are also somewhat buffered from the full financial effect of job loss since they are eligible for military pensions. There is no readily available data source for the fraction of civilian workers who are retirees; there is also no recent evidence that retirees relocate after base closure (the available data sources are not quite current enough to capture post-closure behavior). Therefore, the more military retirees among the civilian workers, the better the community should do.

Last, the attractiveness of the base's facilities and location for alternate uses will obviously have a large effect on the prospects for reuse and, hence, on the longer-run economic prospects for the community. Features such as industrial facilities, housing and airports are commonly mentioned in the plus column, while extensive pollution

---

[4]Bradshaw (1993) estimates that at Castle Air Force Base, 40 percent of military spouses are employed, and that approximately two-thirds of the base's civilian employees are military spouses. The likelihood of spouses leaving the area after base closure is supported by his finding that about 60 percent of civilian workers relocate after closure.

requiring major remediation is usually considered a minus; some observers have looked to remediation as a job creator for the local community, but these jobs are temporary and are a gain only if the funding for remediation comes from an outside source.

## COMMUNITY CHARACTERISTICS

The most direct indicator of a community's vulnerability to a base closure may be the share of total employment or population accounted for by the base. The larger the share of the local community the base represents, the greater will be the effect of the base's closure. This is the primary reason the bases expected to cause the biggest fallout after closure are usually in rural areas or at some remove from major urban areas. Closures of major facilities such as Mare Island or Long Beach may have serious effects on the displaced workers, but the effects on the local community are muted by the fact that the community is embedded in a much larger economy and the workers themselves are spread more widely than is common in more isolated bases.

The relative share of a community's population employed on-base is, of course, not the only relevant factor. The degree to which bases rely on purchases of local goods and services will condition the community-level effects. Indeed, these two factors may operate in different directions depending upon the size of the community. Whereas on-base employment may, ceteris paribus, constitute a larger share of total population in smaller communities, most smaller communities are likely to provide little in the way of goods and services to the base per se.

Community vulnerability is also sensitive to the presence of a school on the base and the age distribution of dependent populations; the greater the fraction of the local school population accounted for by military dependents, the greater the loss in governmental funding after those children leave the district. This loss could be severe if the military children made up a significant fraction of enrollment in the local school district.[5]

---

[5] A recent study suggests that only about 60 percent of per pupil expenditures is directly related to classroom activities (teachers' salaries and materials) and, thus, is

Another age-related issue is the presence in the community of military retirees (regardless of whether they work on the base or not). As was true for those civilian workers who were retirees, military retirees residing in the base community consume health and hospital services on the base if there is an on-post hospital and divert some of their purchases from the local economy to the base. After closure, these retirees are insured under the CHAMPUS system and shift their demand for health services to local hospitals and clinics. Table 2.1 compares the number of retirees and their dependents residing in the local communities around the three bases selected for this study to the number of active duty military and their dependents. In each case, the retiree population is a sizable share of the active military population—ranging from 30 percent for George AFB to over 50 percent for Ft. Ord. The more retirees in the area, the more this increase in hospital demand and other retail business creates additional local economic activity. This effect could be compounded by any hospital job vacancies created by departing military spouses.

The underlying growth trends of the local community clearly affect the nature of the adjustment process, as will general business cycle

Table 2.1

Active Duty and Retiree Populations in Base Communities

|  | Active + Dependents | Retirees + Dependents | Retiree Population as % of Active Population |
|---|---|---|---|
| George AFB | 16,551 | 4,896 | 30 |
| Castle AFB | 16,308 | 6,443 | 40 |
| Fort Ord | 31,412 | 16,351 | 52 |

SOURCES: Data are from impact analyses for each base. Figures for George AFB are for 1989; the figures for Castle AFB and Fort Ord are for 1991. Since the George and Castle AFB studies did not enumerate retirees' dependents, these figures are from the DEERS database, supplied by the Defense Manpower Data Center.

---

readily adjusted when state-level revenues are reduced. Of the remaining 40 percent, 10 percent is spent for district operations and 30 percent for school but not classroom activities. Thus, the reductions in revenues associated with declines in school enrollment are not readily translated into commensurate reductions in costs—at least in the short-run (Krop, Carroll, and Ross, 1995).

effects. As with displacement from any source, displaced workers will be more readily absorbed in a growing economy than in a stagnant or recessionary one. Even communities with bases have other strengths and weaknesses that help to determine the prospects for the local economy, whether these factors are tourism, agriculture, or housing demand from a nearby metropolitan area. While the base closure may alter some of these trends through changes in perception, it seems reasonable to assume that the area's other traits remain a major factor after closure.

Chapter Three
# STUDY PLAN

An overall assessment of the economic impacts of base closures would ideally estimate the effects on the local community as a function of the relevant base and community characteristics. Given the small number of bases that have actually closed, the recency of these closures, the absence of some of the required base data, and the paucity of data about subcounty communities, such a study is not practical at this point. A more feasible strategy is to use case studies of selected bases to see how communities actually fared when their local base was closed.

As explained above, we expect to see the most severe impacts when the closed base was large relative to the size of the community, when the community is relatively isolated geographically, and, of course, after the base has already closed.[1] Since the actual closure process occurs over several years, all or most of the personnel at the base must have already left in order to be sure that the full impact of the closure has already occurred.

This chapter describes the bases we selected for study and our selection criteria, followed by a profile of the selected bases. Next, it lays out the analytic approach of the study and describes the evaluation measures we used. Finally, it describes the three benchmarks we selected to provide a context in which to assess the effect of the base closures.

---

[1]Although this last point seems self-evident, the fact is that the closure process routinely takes several years to complete and most of the bases named in the three BRAC rounds had yet to completely close. See Table 1.1 and Figure 3.1.

## CASE SELECTION

Consistent with the discussion above, we focused on three criteria when choosing bases for the study: the total number of civilian and military personnel at the base should exceed 5,000; the base should be located outside the state's four major urban centers (Los Angeles, San Francisco, Sacramento and San Diego); and the closure process should be completed or substantially completed. When judged by these criteria, all of the 1993 round of closures were excluded because the closure process at these bases is still in its early stages. In addition, most of the bases to be closed in the first two rounds were excluded either because they are located in one of California's major urban centers or because they employed too few personnel (or both).

Only four bases passed these initial screens:

- George AFB, located in Victorville in San Bernardino County
- Norton AFB, located in the City of San Bernardino
- Castle AFB, located primarily in the unincorporated area of Merced County
- Fort Ord, located in the cities of Seaside and Marina in Monterey County.

Rather than select two bases in the same county (San Bernardino), we excluded Norton AFB. George AFB was a better candidate for two primary reasons. First, it has been closed for a longer period than any of the other bases and, unlike Norton, which is located in the city of San Bernardino, it is located at some distance from an urban center. Although Castle AFB is not yet completely closed, the closure process has been well under way there since 1994. Figure 3.1 shows the change in base employment over the last five years; note that Castle AFB still employed workers in 1994.

## PROFILE OF BASES SELECTED

### George Air Force Base

George AFB was established in 1941 in the Mojave Desert in southwestern San Bernardino County in an area known as the Victor Valley

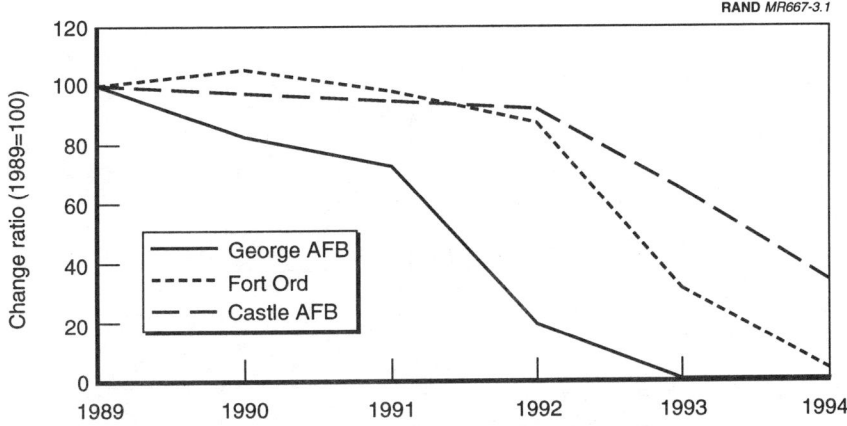

Figure 3.1—Base Employment, 1989–1994

(see Figure 3.2). The base's primary role was the 831st Air Division Headquarters, home of the 35th Tactical Training Wing and the 37th Tactical Training Wing.

The base is located approximately 60 miles from downtown Los Angeles in the rapidly suburbanizing outskirts of the Los Angeles metropolitan area. The neighboring cities of Victorville, Apple Valley, and Hesperia all experienced very rapid growth between 1970 and 1990.[2] (These three cities averaged 140 percent growth between 1970 and 1980 and 244 percent growth between 1980 and 1990.) George AFB is also located within a 50-mile radius of three other Air Force bases (Edwards AFB, located approximately 25 miles northwest, Norton AFB, approximately 35 miles southeast, and March AFB, approximately 50 miles south). Norton AFB is scheduled for closure and March AFB has been realigned (downsized). The base was designated for closure in December 1988 and was closed on December 15, 1992.

George AFB was the largest employer in the Victor Valley, although a sizable fraction of the population commutes to work in the neighbor-

---

[2]The 1990 population of those cities was Apple Valley 46,000, Hesperia 50,000, and Victorville 41,000.

18    The Effects of Military Base Closures on Local Communities

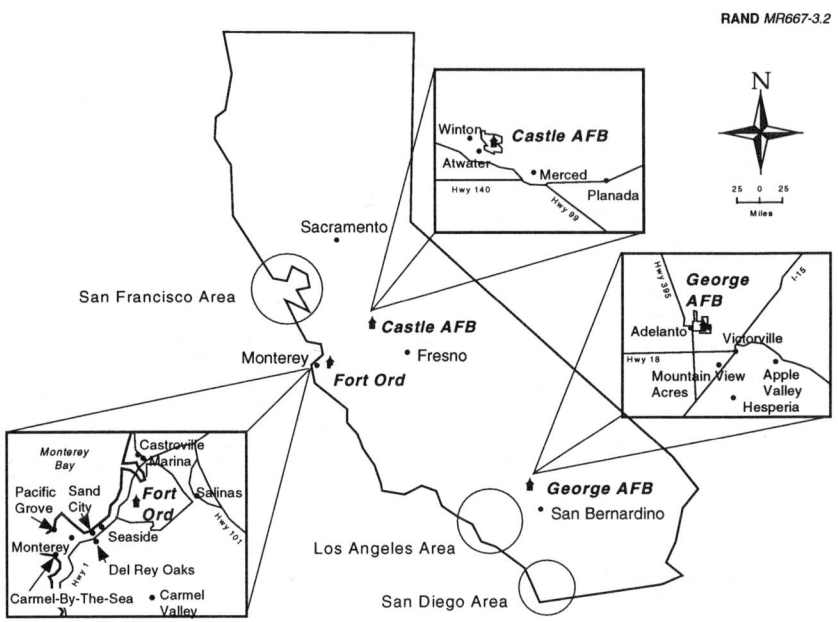

Figure 3.2—Location of Bases Selected for Study

ing Los Angeles metropolitan area. Jobs in construction and service sector employment predominate among nonmilitary employment in the Victor Valley. About half of the military personnel and associated dependents at George AFB lived off base in 1989.

## Fort Ord

Fort Ord is located in northern Monterey County, adjacent to Monterey Bay, on California's Central Coast (see Figure 3.2). It was the home of the Army's 7th Infantry Division and was designated as a major training center, which was used extensively during the Vietnam War. Fort Ord also provided support and administrative services to other military facilities in the region, including Fort Hunter Liggett, the Presidio of Monterey (which houses the Defense Language Institute), the Naval Postgraduate School, and a Coast Guard station.

Ord was slated for closure in 1991 and eventually closed three years later on September 30, 1994. The military retained part of the base for housing staff and students at the Defense Language Institute and the Naval Postgraduate School. About 15 percent of the military and civilian personnel lived off base, primarily in the adjoining cities of Marina, Monterey, Salinas, and Pacific Grove.

The communities in the immediate vicinity of the base represent a very diverse mix of places. Directly adjoining the base are the two moderately sized communities of Seaside (to the south) and Marina (to the north). Seaside's population has basically been stable since 1970 and in 1990 stood at 39,000. Marina grew rapidly during the 1970s (147 percent growth) but more modestly during the 1980s (28 percent) and totaled 26,000 in 1990. Employment in both of these communities was heavily weighted toward services and sales. Just south of Seaside is the city of Del Rey Oaks, a very small residential community primarily occupied by military related personnel. A little farther south is Monterey, the county seat, at one time a major food processing center but increasingly a tourist center. Monterey's population in 1990 was 32,000, having grown modestly (16 percent) between 1980 and 1990.

Farther to the east is Salinas, the largest city in the county (110,000 in 1990) and a major agricultural processing center for this agriculturally rich county. Salinas experienced considerable growth between 1970 and 1990, averaging 35 percent growth per decade. Fort Ord's presence in Monterey county added another element to what was already one of the most disparate counties in the state—combining the affluent retirement and recreation centers of Carmel and the Monterey peninsula, the increasingly professional population of Monterey, the more blue collar communities of Seaside and Marina, and the growing agricultural center of Salinas.

## Castle Air Force Base

Castle AFB is located in Central California's Merced county, in the heart of California's San Joaquin Valley (see Figure 3.2). From 1946 to 1992, Castle AFB was a Strategic Air Command base. The Air Combat Command assumed control of the base in June 1992. BRAC announced closure in 1991 but the base is not expected to close fully until later in 1995. Approximately 65 percent of the uniformed personnel had left by October 1994.

To the immediate west of Castle AFB is the small community of Winton (1990 population of 7,600), to the southwest is the community of Atwater (1990 population of 22,000), and approximately 5 miles to the southwest is the city of Merced, the county seat, with a population of 56,000. All three communities experienced moderate to rapid growth during the 1970s (an average of 53 percent) and 1980s (an average of 44 percent). Employment in these communities is concentrated in manufacturing (food products, printing and publishing, and aluminum processing), services (health care and insurance), and agriculture (livestock and poultry). It is one of California's poorest counties in terms of per capita income.

## ANALYTICAL APPROACH

For the purposes of this study, we defined the local community to be the "local impact area" as defined by each base's Reuse Authority.[3] Two aspects of our analytical approach need to be discussed: first, the measures used to evaluate the effects of base closure and, second, the benchmarks used to evaluate those effects.

### Evaluation Measures

Although base closures can affect host communities in a wide variety of ways, in fact, most studies of the process focus on three general categories or mechanisms of effects: changes that result from reductions in population, changes that are transmitted through declines in employment, and changes that are felt through a reduction in housing demand.[4]

---

[3]See Appendix C for a list of zip codes included in each community. Fort Ord's local impact area was examined both with and without Salinas. Although Salinas is technically part of the Ord impact area, in fact its connections with Fort Ord are less direct than the other communities. Moreover, presenting the comparison with and without Salinas provides an indication of how localized the effects of base closure may be.

[4]See for example, U.S. Department of Defense (1994), California Military Base Reuse Task Force (1994), Commission on State Finance (1990), Innes et al. (1994).

Each of these mechanisms can, of course, produce a diverse array of compounding effects. The direct impact of reductions in employment, for example, are felt most by the individuals who lose their jobs and associated earnings. The community may in turn feel the direct impact of this in the form of reduced total employment and higher unemployment rates. This direct loss of employment and earnings may also be felt in a variety of indirect ways: the closing of businesses that relied on the patronage of base personnel, a decline in retail sales and, correspondingly, sales tax revenues in the community, an increased need for services to the newly unemployed, and so on.[5]

Similarly, population losses sustained as military personnel and their dependents leave the community will reduce school enrollments and (since state aid to local schools is based on total enrollment) the revenues used to support the schools. This, in turn, might result in layoffs of school personnel and thus further compound the effects of the base closure. Finally, as personnel who live in the local housing market leave the area, this will reduce the demand for housing with associated effects on vacancy rates, market values, and housing construction activity.

In sum, the effects of base closure can be classified in terms of three general categories of change. Correspondingly, our analysis utilizes a basic set of measures (shown in Table 3.1) that attempt to capture

Table 3.1

**Measures**

| Population Changes | Employment Effects | Housing Effects |
|---|---|---|
| Size of change | Size of labor force | Number of units |
| Drop in school enrollments | Unemployment rate | Vacancy rates |
| | Taxable retail sales | Sale prices |
| | Municipal revenues | |

---

[5]In general, the size of these indirect effects is likely to vary with the size of the multiplier effect of military spending in the local area. As Innes et al. (1994) suggest, many estimates of this effect may be exaggerated. Their review of the existing literature suggests that 1.2 to 1.4 is likely to bound the true figure (i.e., for each direct base job lost, another 0.2 to 0.4 jobs is lost due to indirect effects). This compares with some multiplier estimates of 3 or even 4.

these three basic factors. Specifically, we focus on two measures of population change in the local area (the size of the local population and the change in school enrollments), four measures of direct and indirect employment effects (size of the labor force, unemployment rates, taxable retail sales, and municipal revenues), and three housing measures (the number of housing units, the vacancy rate, and sales prices of owner-occupied housing).

## Benchmarks for Comparisons

The first step in our analysis is to describe how the measures discussed above have behaved prior to and after the closure of the selected bases. This description focuses on what actually occurred without reference to any particular standard against which to evaluate these changes. Such before–after comparisons are the starting point for our analysis. However, they fail to provide a context or standard with which to assess change. They ignore, for example, both the broad-scale and more local changes that may have affected the local area, independent of the base closure.

Before–after comparisons also fail to take into account the fact that local and state officials will employ some benchmark (whether implicitly or explicitly) to evaluate both the severity of the base closure's effects on the local communities and whether these communities will need special assistance to adjust to the closure. Thus, to place what actually happened in context and to assess its significance, it is useful to employ a benchmark against which to measure the actual change.

Several alternative benchmarks might be employed. In one sense, the impact of the base closure is most completely gauged in terms of what would have happened to the community if the base had not closed. However, it is impossible to measure this counterfactual. Instead, we employ three different benchmarks in this analysis, each designed to evaluate the actual changes from a particular perspective. The benchmarks are the following:

- Comparison with predicted effects
- Comparison with similar bases that did not close
- Comparison with other communities in same county

The first of these benchmarks compares the actual change with what had been predicted in the various studies done to estimate the effects of closure prior to its occurrence.[6] This benchmark answers the question: How did the effects of base closure compare with what the local community (or their consultants) expected? Although such projections are sometimes criticized for their political motivations, projections done by the Congressional Budget Office and the military services don't often fall into this category. Whatever their inherent limitations, however, policymakers would still be required to compare projected versus actual outcomes to determine if some type of transition assistance might be required.

The second set of comparisons adopts a different perspective. It compares the experience at each of the three bases with a matched set of California bases that have not been scheduled for closure. Although each base obviously has unique features that make a completely matched comparison impossible, the three alternative bases have been chosen to match as closely as possible the three closed bases. This benchmark addresses the question: What might have happened had the three bases selected for our analysis not closed?

The final set of comparisons focuses on how the experience in the communities most affected by the base closures compares with other communities in the same counties. This benchmark attempts to hold constant general regional trends and asks the question: How does the experience of the communities directly affected by the closures differ from that of the county as a whole?

---

[6]At each of the three bases examined in this analysis, preclosure studies predicted the effects of the eventual closure. See Appendix A and Appendix B.

Chapter Four
# ANALYSIS

## BASIC DESCRIPTION

Figure 4.1 plots the pattern of total population change in each of the local impact areas affected by the base closures between 1981 and 1994. In each case, the population levels are indexed to the area's 1981 population. Thus, values of 100 indicate that the population has remained at 1981 levels, whereas values greater than 100 indicate the rate of population growth in subsequent years. These measures are plotted for four different impact areas: one each for George and Castle AFBs and two for Fort Ord—one including and one excluding the city of Salinas. The figure also identifies the years in which the

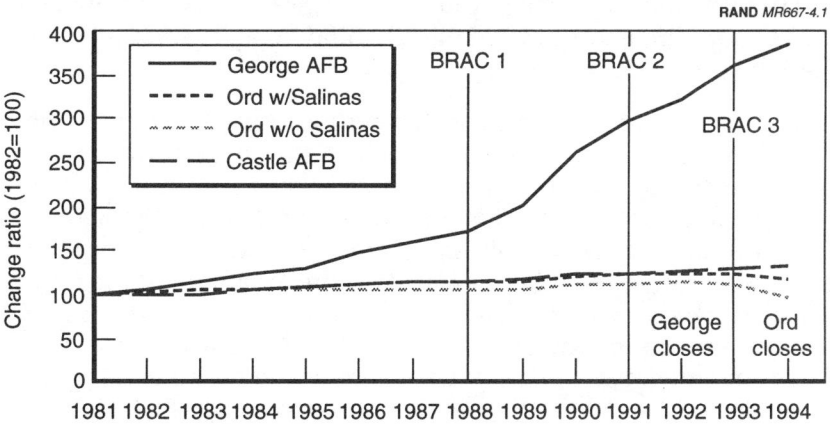

Figure 4.1—Population Trends, 1981–1994

different BRAC cuts were announced[1] and the year in which George and Ord were finally closed.

The patterns of population change differ sharply across the impact areas. The pattern of growth observed in the Victor Valley, in which George is located, has clearly diverged from the patterns in the Ord and Castle areas. The rapid population growth that was evident well before the closure of George was announced does not appear to have abated. Indeed, the rate of growth between 1988, when the closure was announced, and 1992, when George was finally closed, appears to have accelerated—a trend that has continued through 1994. As we noted in our previous description of George, the Victor Valley has been one of the most rapidly growing areas of California—a by-product of the rapid movement of people from Los Angeles County to the less expensive housing available in San Bernardino County. The closure of George does not seem to have even slowed this trend.

Although the pattern of change around Ord and Castle is much less dramatic, the principal impression one draws from this figure is one of stability or even modest growth rather than decline. The communities around Castle, for example, have actually experienced some very modest growth, and the population in the Fort Ord impact area remained very stable until 1994, when the base actually closed. Moreover, when Salinas is added to the area, the actual decline is very modest, suggesting that the population impact of closure in the Ord impact area may be highly localized. It should also be noted that the Fort Ord impact area was falling behind in population relative to the Salinas area since 1986.

Figure 4.2 compares the rates of changes for a broader range of measures between 1989 and 1994 in each of the impact areas. Once again the comparison is drawn separately for the Ord impact area with and without Salinas. This comparison once again highlights the very different experience of the communities around George AFB and those around the other bases. With the exception of the unemployment rate, which appears to have climbed slightly higher around George than around the other bases, the picture one draws from the data is one of growth. This pattern is reflected in the total popula-

---

[1]The closure of George AFB was announced in the first round of BRAC cuts. The closure of Castle and Ord were announced in the second round.

Analysis 27

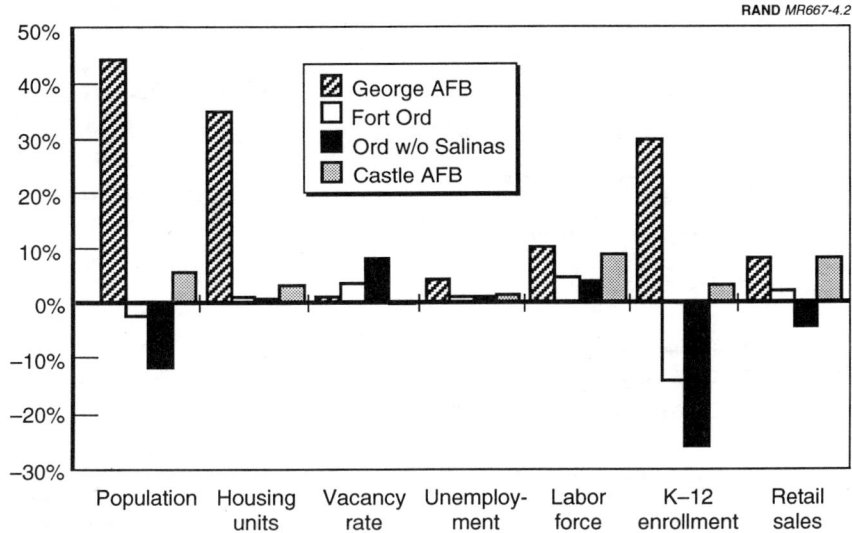

Figure 4.2—Community Changes Since Base Closure

tion, housing unit, labor force, school enrollment, and retail sales figures.

The pattern is decidedly more mixed in the areas surrounding Castle and Ord. In the Castle impact area the picture that emerges is one of stability and modest growth; this is reflected in the small increases in population, housing stock, labor force, school enrollment, and retail sales. Although the rate of unemployment climbed slightly, this period was one of recession and rising unemployment in the state of California in general. The changes around Ord, by far the largest of the three bases, are less positive. The population has declined, vacancy rates have increased, school enrollment has dropped sharply, retail sales are off, and unemployment has edged up slightly. These effects, however, appear to be substantially more pronounced for the circumscribed definition of the Ord impact area than for the area including Salinas.

Figures 4.3, 4.4, and 4.5 provide a third view of trends by looking at how sales prices of single family homes have changed in the impact areas between the announcement of impending closure and 1994.

28  The Effects of Military Base Closures on Local Communities

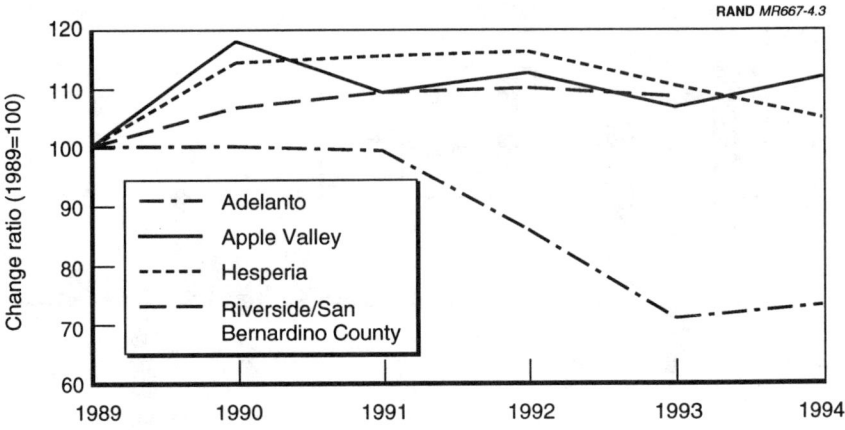

Figure 4.3—Housing Prices Around George AFB

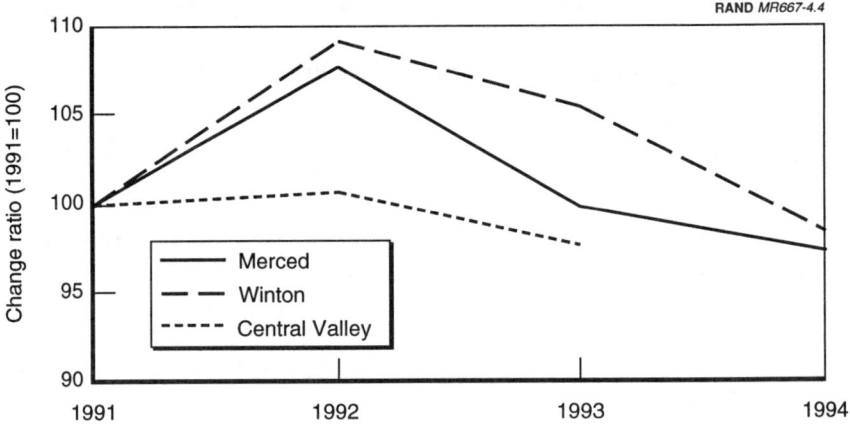

Figure 4.4—Housing Prices Around Castle AFB

Where available, the data are presented for individual jurisdictions. These more detailed data enable us to compare trends within the impact areas.[2]

_____

[2]Note that the scale of Figures 4.4 and 4.5 is much smaller than that in Figure 4.3, since the magnitudes of housing price changes around Castle AFB and Fort Ord were much smaller than those around George AFB.

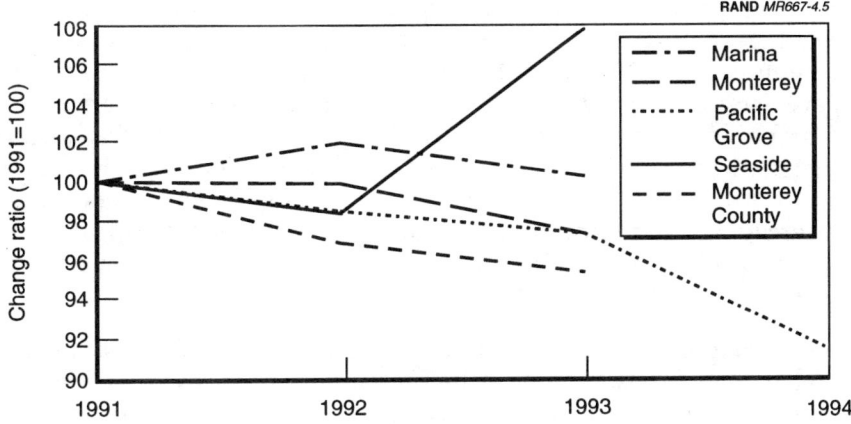

Figure 4.5—Housing Prices Around Fort Ord

From the previous comparisons, we might expect the trends in the Victor Valley to be more positive than in the other two areas. These communities experienced substantial population and housing growth prior to, during, and after the closure process. Indeed, Figure 4.3 shows that market values (indexed on 1989 values) have generally risen since the closure was announced. The pattern of this increase, however, is neither monotonic nor universal. After an initial rise between 1989 and 1990, market values seem to have fluctuated within a relatively narrow range, although remaining higher than at the beginning of the period.

The one exception to this pattern is Adelanto, the community directly adjacent to George. Here market values remained stable for two years before plunging sharply as the final closure neared. This decline, however, appears to have stopped in the first full year after the closure (1994) and may have actually risen. Although Adelanto's proximity to the base was no doubt a factor in this decline in home values, it is also important to note that between 1991 and 1994 the housing stock in Adelanto increased by almost 60 percent. Thus, the 30-percent decline in Adelanto during this period may have been particularly sharp because at the same time that the military was moving out, the housing stock was expanding dramatically.

Housing prices around Castle (Figure 4.4) have also followed an irregular path during this period. After initially rising almost 10 percent in the year following announcement of the closure, sales prices gave back all of that increase in the two succeeding years. As a result, market values at the end of the period where approximately where they had begun three years earlier. Although the pattern is clearly more erratic in the two communities for which we have sales data (Merced city and Winton), the overall pattern does not appear to be dramatically different from the pattern for the central valley as a whole.

Finally, Figure 4.5 compares trends in sales prices in the Ord impact area. With the exception of the city of Seaside, these data show a relatively consistent trend across communities. Sales prices have generally declined—albeit at a modest rate—throughout the closure period. As a result, prices ended up somewhat lower at the end than at the beginning of the period.

The pattern for Seaside is somewhat anomalous. After dropping by about 2 percent between 1991 and 1992 housing prices climbed approximately 10 percentage points between 1992 and 1993. It is difficult to know what to make of this pattern, since Seaside abuts Fort Ord and has traditionally housed a sizable portion of the civilian and off-base military personnel. It may be that the largest declines in value took place in the rental housing market (for which comparable data are not available).

Judging simply by a comparison of the behavior of the measures used here, it appears that the effects of base closures have varied rather dramatically across the three areas we have chosen.[3] On virtually every indicator we examined, the area surrounding George AFB appears to have experienced little negative change. Instead, most indicators have changed in the positive direction, and in some cases very sharply. The principal reason for this seems to be continued and perhaps even accelerated suburban expansion from Los Angeles County. While the picture from the Castle impact area is not as bright, most of the indicator variables show stability or even modest

---

[3]It is useful to keep in mind that these areas were purposely chosen because we expected them to be especially prone to feel the effects of base closure, and we expected those effects to be readily observable.

growth rather than decline. Only around Fort Ord are the trends less positive. But even here, some indicators have improved and the most pronounced downward movements appear to have been concentrated in the communities immediately surrounding the base.

## COMPARISON WITH PROJECTIONS

In the interim between the initial release of the list of bases being considered for closure and the BRAC's submission of its final recommendations to the president and Congress, it is standard procedure for local communities and other interested parties to prepare estimates of the consequences of individual base closures. Although the methodologies, sophistication, and level of effort of these studies vary enormously (see Bradshaw, 1993), these estimates often shape the expectations and/or fears of local community leaders and provide a basis for trying to influence the BRAC's decision. They also provide us with a benchmark against which to measure the change that actually occurs.

Figure 4.6 compares actual and projected changes in four of our indicators for the George AFB impact area.[4] On each of the four measures, the actual experience was more positive than the projection. The fact that the projected totals on three of these four measures are either positive or essentially neutral presumably reflects that the projections were made in light of the underlying growth of this area. These differences are particularly pronounced for the school enrollment measures, both of which refer to subareas within the larger impact area and, thus, might be expected to be more significantly affected than the entire impact area. The projection for elementary school enrollment in Adelanto, the community adjacent to George, for example, was for a 50-percent drop in enrollment. In fact, enrollment dropped a little more than 10 percent.

A similar pattern is apparent in the Castle impact area (see Figure 4.7). While unemployment rose in this area, the actual increase was less than half what had been projected. Moreover, whereas the local

---

[4]The sources of these projections are abbreviated within parentheses under the graphs in Figures 4.6–4.8. For more information about the sources, see Appendix A.

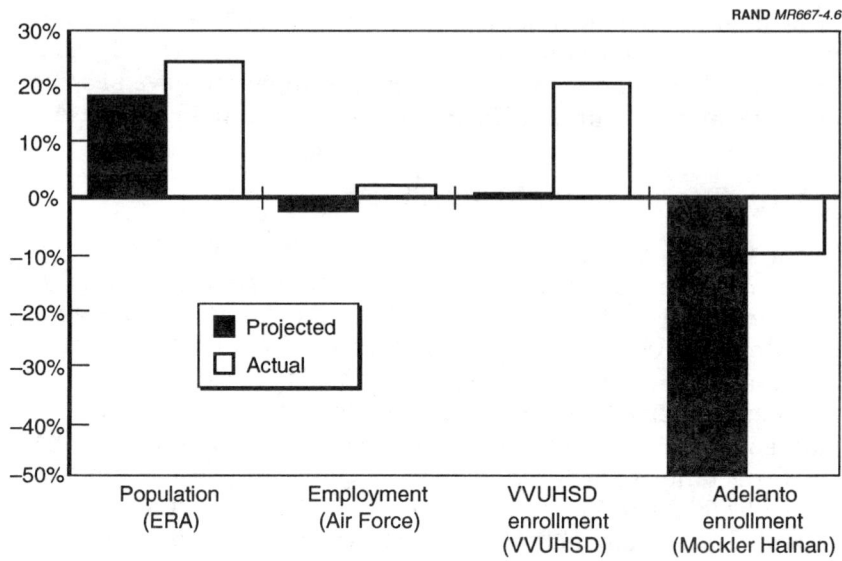

Figure 4.6—Projected Versus Actual Changes, George AFB

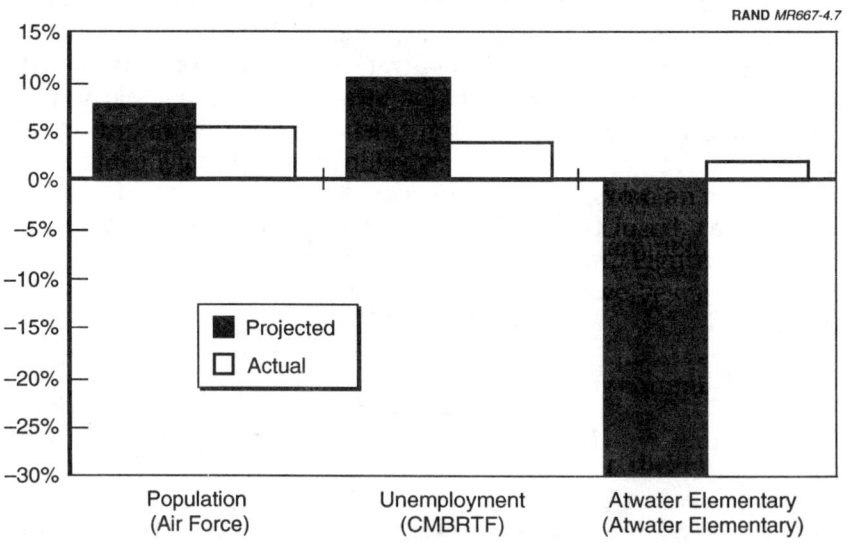

Figure 4.7—Projected Versus Actual Changes, Castle AFB

school district had projected a 30-percent drop in elementary school enrollment, enrollment actually inched up somewhat. The only measure in which the actual change was less positive than projected was total population growth, and here the difference between actual and projected levels was very small.

Although the actual change that occurred in the Ord impact area was more negative than in either of the other two base impact areas, the difference between projected and actual levels was in the same direction (see Figure 4.8). In other words, on each measure, the projected situation was worse than what actually transpired.[5] The school enrollment projections and city revenues were reasonably accurate, but the forecasts for population, unemployment, and retail sales anticipated far worse outcomes than actually occurred.

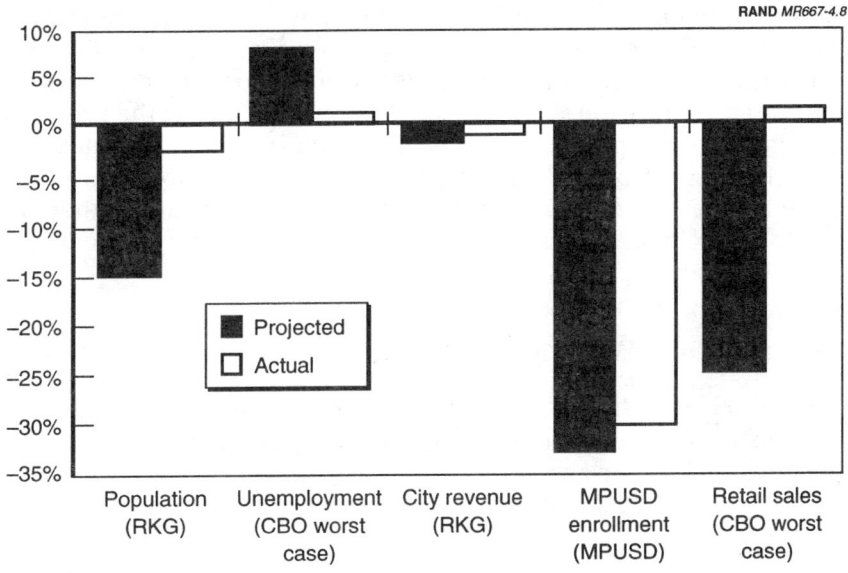

Figure 4.8—Projected Versus Actual Changes, Fort Ord

---

[5]Note that the definition of community in both the projected and actual cases is the entire area defined by the Reuse Authority.

Overall, the actual impact of base closure on each of these three areas appears to have been decidedly less dramatic than was projected. Although, as mentioned above, the level of sophistication and effort that went into these projections varies considerably, the general point remains that the actual impact was better than expected. This, in turn, suggests that fears of local community leaders may be exaggerated. It also raises the possibility that the methodologies used to make these projections may be problematic.[6]

Indeed, these comparisons highlight the importance of monitoring what actually occurs in local communities subsequent to base closure. While community-sponsored projections may well be faulted for the fact that they are often generated as part of community efforts to reverse the initial BRAC recommendations for base closure, policymakers will nonetheless be subject to political pressures to mitigate the effects of those closures. Barring efforts to monitor what has actually occurred, policymakers will have little information on which to base their decisions about providing special assistance to mitigate such projected effects. In fact, as the previous discussion of the potential effects of base closure demonstrates, the actual effects of closure are much less straightforward than many communities assume. Monitoring the short-term changes that actually occur in local communities provides a necessary benchmark for policymakers.

## COMPARISON WITH MATCHED BASES

As we discussed above, the most appropriate standard for measuring the effects of base closure is to compare what actually occurred with what would have occurred had the base not closed. This, of course, is impossible.[7] Instead, we have attempted to approximate this

---

[6]This point is suggested both by Innes et al. (1994) and U.S. Department of Defense (1994), who indicate that the most problematic element of these projections lies in the estimated employment multipliers used in the projections.

[7]Given a more complete model of the effects of base closure and the data necessary to estimate such a model, we might, in fact, be able to generate more complete estimates of what might have occurred in local communities had the bases not closed. However, since relatively few bases have, in fact, closed, since we lack a fully specified model of those effects, and since the required time series data do not exist, there is no way to generate such estimates.

comparison by matching each of the three bases in our sample with a comparable base in California that remains open. Since no two bases are identical, matching bases is more a matter of degree than a simple binary choice. Consistent with our hypothesis about where the effects of closure are likely to be greatest,[8] we have used three criteria to select matches.

- The bases should be in the same service or at least perform relatively similar functions.
- The bases should have roughly similar numbers of personnel and employees.
- The bases should be outside of a major urban center.

Although California has a large number of military installations, it is impossible to select a very close match for the closed bases. Nonetheless, the bases we did select provide a reasonable approximation.

The matched pairs for our comparisons are Vandenberg AFB and George AFB, Camp Pendleton and Fort Ord, and Beale AFB and Castle AFB. The Vandenberg–George and Beale–Castle pairs link bases of roughly similar size, run by the same service, and located in similar types of areas (on the fringe of major metropolitan areas in the case of Vandenberg–George and in California's Central Valley in the case of Beale–Castle). The Pendleton–Ord pair is somewhat more of a stretch since Pendleton is more than twice as large as Ord and the bases are run by different services. However, both bases served a major infantry training function (Ord for the army; Pendleton for the marines), both are located on the California coastline, and both are some distance from a major urban center.[9]

In all three cases, the open base (in terms of military and civilian personnel) comprises a larger fraction of the local impact area popula-

---

[8]As noted earlier, we assume that the effects of base closures are likely to be greatest where the base is relatively large, especially with respect to its surrounding area, and when it is located outside of a major urban center.

[9]Camp Pendleton is located in San Diego County, which makes this comparison somewhat problematic; however, Pendleton and the city of San Diego are located at opposite ends of the county.

tion than the closed bases.[10] As a result, we might expect the open bases to have a relatively larger effect on their local areas than the bases that closed. (Holding other economic characteristics constant, we would expect each of the open bases' communities to suffer greater impacts from base closure than the three closed bases being studied here.)

Finally, the matched pairs differ in the background rate of growth of the counties in which they are located. San Bernardino and Merced, for example, grew considerably faster than Santa Barbara (Vandenberg) and Yuba (Beale) both before and after the base closures; the reverse is true for Monterey and San Diego. This last point is important since, as a general rule, we would expect the open bases to score higher than the closed bases on our indicator variables, but this may not be the case if background developments in the county dominate the trends in the local impact areas.

Figure 4.9, which compares patterns of change in the indicator measures for the George and Vandenberg local impact areas, suggests that such background factors do indeed dominate this comparison. Ordinarily, as noted above, we would expect the values for the open base (Vandenberg) to exceed those for the closed base (George), but the exact reverse of the expected pattern is observed in this figure. Indeed, these data would lead one to believe that Vandenberg was the base that had been closed instead of George. What this indicates, of course, is that the rapid movement of suburbanizing residents into the Victor Valley of San Bernardino overwhelms the impact of the base closing. While it is true that absent the closing of George this growth might have been even more dramatic, the difference would have been only a matter of degree.

The comparisons between Beale and Castle (Figure 4.10) and Pendleton and Ord (Figure 4.11) follow the more expected pattern. In both cases, the indicator variables changed in a more positive direction in the open than the closed bases. In the case of Beale and Castle the difference is a matter of degree; in the case of Pendleton and Ord it is

---

[10]Vandenberg's personnel constitutes 16 percent of the impact area versus 5 percent for George; Beale's personnel are 14 percent versus 8 percent for Castle; and Pendleton's personnel represent 21 percent versus 8 percent for Ord.

Analysis 37

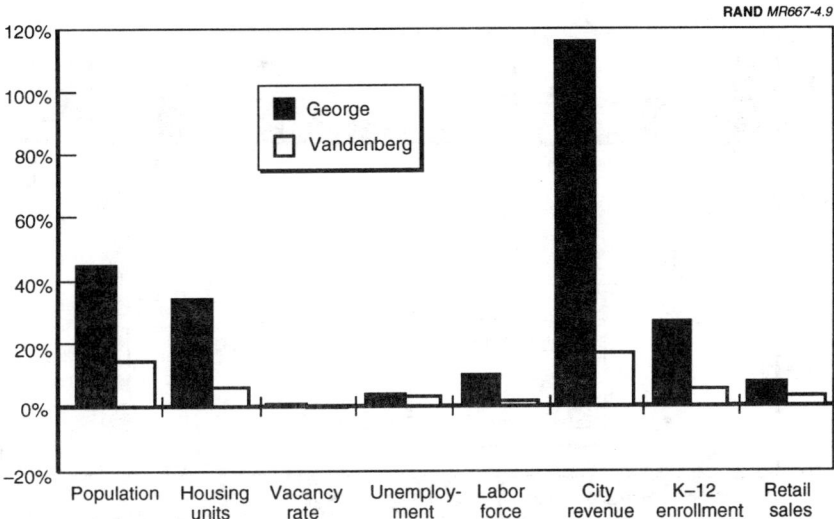

Figure 4.9—George AFB Versus Vandenberg AFB, 1989–1994 Changes

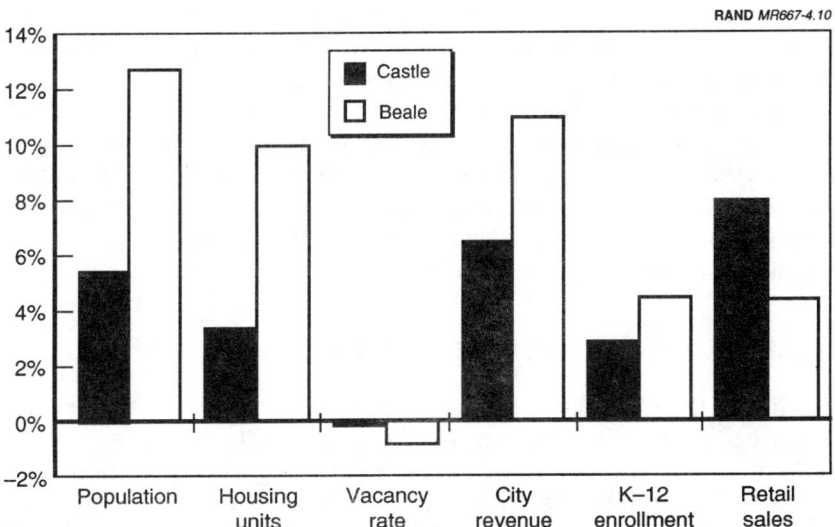

Figure 4.10—Castle AFB Versus Beale AFB, 1991–1994 Changes

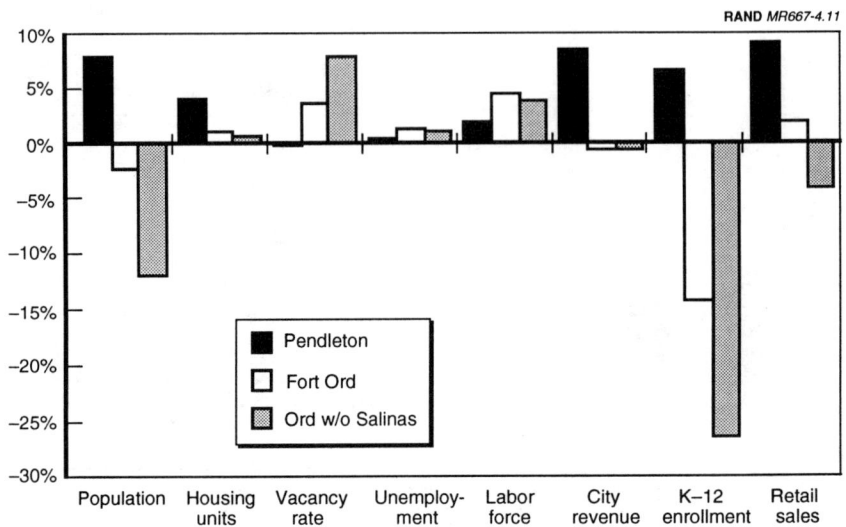

Figure 4.11—Fort Ord Versus Camp Pendleton, 1991–1994 Changes

often also a matter of direction.[11] Although it is impossible, given the differences between bases, to know what would have happened in the affected communities had the bases not closed, these comparisons suggest that in general, the situation would have been more positive. It is impossible to know, however, how large those differences would have been. Moreover, it seems clear from these comparisons that, apart from the situation on the bases, the underlying trends in the region and its economy will play a much larger role in shaping the effects of base closure.

## COMPARISON WITH COUNTY TOTALS

Studies of the base closure process have suggested that the effects of closure are typically localized—centered in the communities in proximity to the base (cited in Bradshaw, 1993). Indeed, the comparisons of the Fort Ord impact area with and without Salinas lend some credence to this point. In this section we provide additional supporting

---

[11] Several of the indicator variables are negative for Ord but positive for Pendleton.

evidence by comparing our basic indicator measures in the local impact area with the identical measures for the counties in which they are located. To the extent that the base closure effects are highly localized, we would expect to find the county-level measures to have a better score than the local impact area (whether positive or negative) on each dimension. In addition, to the extent that the county scores reflect broader regional trends that influence what is happening in the local impact area independent of the closure, that may also be reflected in these data.

Figure 4.12 compares the pattern in the George AFB local impact area with the patterns in San Bernardino County. Contrary to our expectations, we find that the George AFB local impact area has done even better on most of these measures than the county as a whole. The only measures for which this does not hold are the vacancy and unemployment rates, and in both of these cases the differences are very small. Since the Victor Valley impact area contains slightly less than 10 percent of the total residents of San Bernardino County, it is unlikely that the county totals are shaped to any significant degree by

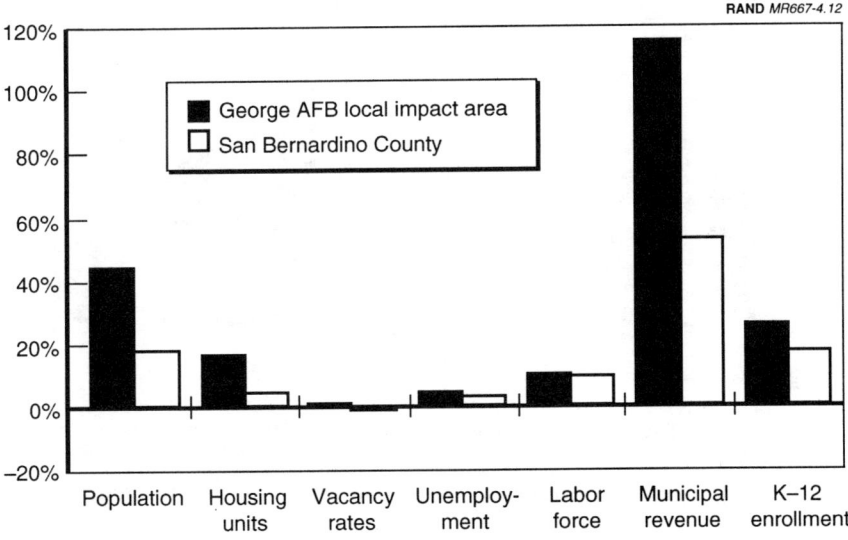

Figure 4.12—George AFB Versus San Bernardino County, 1989–1994

the pattern in the George impact area.[12] The generally positive values on these measures for the county as a whole reflect the fact that San Bernardino County is among the fastest growing areas of California. Thus, these data suggest that, despite the closure of George AFB, the George impact area is leading rather than lagging behind the growth occurring in San Bernardino County.

The pattern is somewhat different in the Castle local impact area (Figure 4.13). The Castle impact area contains about 45 percent of the total Merced County population; thus, Castle's impact area will have a larger impact on the aggregate county totals than George's impact area will have on San Bernardino County. Overall, Merced County's scores on these measures, although generally positive, lag substantially behind those for San Bernardino County. Moreover, the county has more positive scores on these measures than does the local impact area. The only exceptions to this are labor force growth

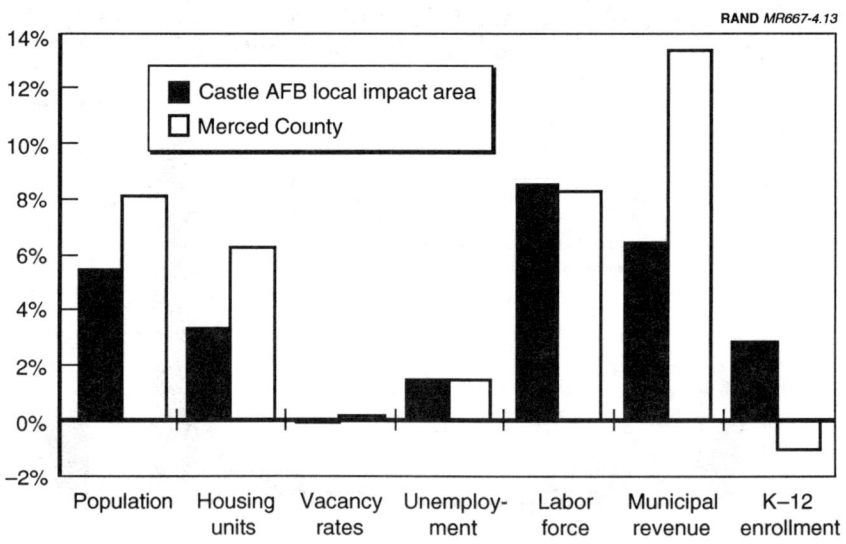

Figure 4.13—Castle AFB Versus Merced County, 1991–1994

---

[12]Moreover, San Bernardino County is the largest county in area in the United States.

and K–12 enrollment. This pattern conforms more closely to the expected pattern, with the immediate impact area lagging behind the wider region in which it is located. As pointed out in the basic description section above, it remains true that on all but one of the indicators (unemployment), the values for the local impact area have improved during the closure period.

The expected pattern is even clearer in the Fort Ord local impact area (see Figure 4.14). As in our earlier comparisons, we distinguish the local impact area with and without the city of Salinas. This provides us with an additional level of detail in examining the degree to which the effects of base closures are localized within the larger region. In comparing the Monterey County totals with those of San Bernardino and Merced, it is important to note that the wider local impact area (including Salinas) constitutes almost two-thirds of the total population of the county. Thus, the Monterey County totals are much more heavily influenced by the local impact area than is true in either of the other cases. In light of this, it may not be surprising that Monterey County scores lower on most of these indicator measures than either San Bernardino or Merced. Indeed, the picture that emerges from the Monterey County data is one of very little aggregate change.

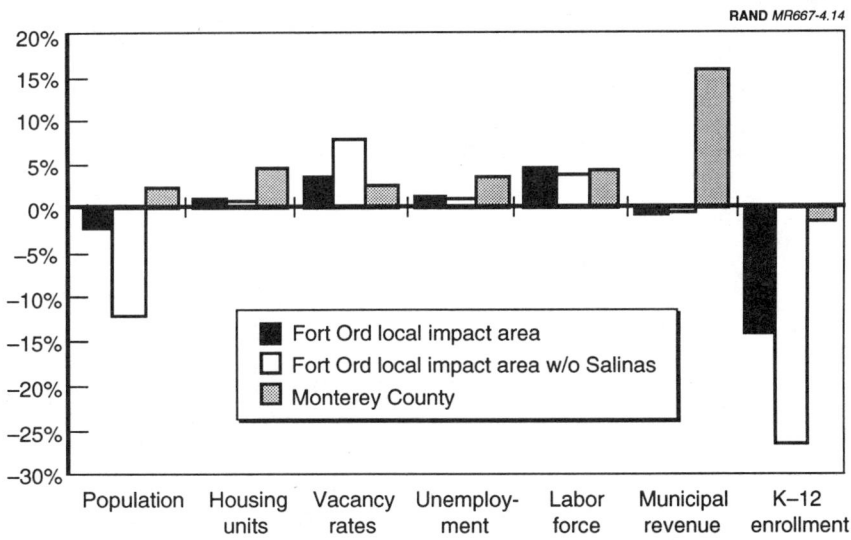

Figure 4.14—Fort Ord Versus Monterey County, 1991–1994

When the comparison focuses on the patterns within the county, the results support the localization of base closure effects. With the exception of the two labor force measures (where the differences are very minor), the Monterey County values are more positive than those for the local impact area—however defined. Moreover, the more narrowly circumscribed the local impact area, the greater is the difference. This pattern offers considerable support for the notion that the impact of base closures is quite localized.

Chapter Five
# RESULTS AND CONCLUSIONS

## RESULTS

The pattern of change followed an idiosyncratic pattern. In one case, the communities surrounding the closed base (George AFB) seem to have prospered before, during, and after the closure. This picture holds regardless of the benchmark used and despite the fact that the communities surrounding this base experienced significant political difficulties in developing and approving a base reuse plan.

In a second case (Castle AFB) the picture that emerges depends, at least in part, on which measures and benchmarks are chosen. On most measures, the observed changes were small—sometimes positive and sometimes negative—but on two of the three benchmarks (versus a matched set of communities and versus the county as a whole), the communities failed to perform as well as the standard. The fact that about one-third of Castle's base personnel remained in October of 1994 may have contributed to these findings.

In the third case (Fort Ord) the picture is generally less positive. On most measures and across most benchmarks the effects are more consistently negative. However, the magnitude of these effects appears to relate directly to which communities are included in the definition of the local impact area. The more narrowly that area is defined, the more negative the measured impact, suggesting that even here the effects of base closure are localized.

The geographic spread of these effects will, of course, be conditioned by the nature of the markets that are affected. In other words, to the extent that local housing and retail service markets are geographically circumscribed (as they most assuredly are), we would expect the impact of base closures to be felt most directly by communities within the local market areas. As one moves beyond the local market area, the impact of base closures is likely to be attenuated. Since, in fact, the range of local markets may well differ across different submarkets (e.g., housing, labor, retail sales), we might well expect the effects of base closure to vary across different submarkets.

One finding that is clear across bases and communities is that the actual effects of base closure appear substantially more benign than those projected in the local impact studies that were done prior to the closures. The seeming unreliability of these projections may stem from what appear to be excessive economic multipliers in the economic models used for the forecasts.

## CONCLUSIONS

The current study aimed to determine how the most recent round of base closures had affected three large, geographically isolated military bases and their surrounding communities. Despite our use both of multiple measures of the effects of closure and multiple standards of comparison, data limitations prevent us from generalizing from these results to other bases that might be closed in the future. Nonetheless, the results of this analysis do agree with the finding of earlier studies that the effects of base closure are highly localized geographically; the recency of these closures, however, prevents us from determining how long-lived these effects may be.

In terms of the specific bases and communities examined, the analysis suggests three general conclusions:

- The effects of base closure are highly localized.
- The larger the base relative to the surrounding communities, the larger are the effects.
- Underlying economic factors—in particular the longer-term pattern of population and economic growth of the local area—seem to condition the overall impact of base closure on the surrounding communities.

In this context, it is important to emphasize that all of these comparisons were made at a time when California was experiencing its most severe recession of the post-war period. Whether these effects would have differed had the closures occurred during a period of economic expansion is an open question. What is clear is that it is very difficult to detect any negative impact of base closure in the area around George AFB that was experiencing strong underlying growth.

One final point deserves mention. In all three cases examined, the actual effects of base closure were far less severe than predicted. This result should sound as a cautionary note when considering forecasts about future base closures. Technical choices about the multipliers to use and the compensating factors to consider will clearly affect the results of such forecasts. As we noted above, several mitigating factors can offset the effects of base closure. Among these are the following:

- the withdrawal of working spouses from the local labor market
- double counting of spouses who are employed as civilian base workers
- the attenuated financial impact of military personnel who live on the base due to the economic isolation from the community
- the redirection of retirees' retail and medical expenditures from the base to the local community (perhaps the most important factor).

Currently, the absence of data makes it impossible to measure the potential effects of these countervailing factors. These data problems span three areas. First, measuring the effects of closure requires a wide array of measures given the complexity of the process. Such data include both the characteristics of bases and base personnel, (e.g., the number of spouses working on- and off-post, the number of civilian employees who are retirees, the expenditures of retirees and their dependents at base hospitals) and of measures of local community outcomes (e.g., retail sales, housing market prices, new job openings). Unfortunately, such data are not routinely collected.

Second, even when data are available for larger spatial units (e.g., counties or metropolitan areas), they are rarely collected for local communities in any kind of systematic fashion. Given what appears to be the localized nature of base closure effects, this lack of local data makes it very difficult to determine just what the extent of those effects might be.

Finally, the timing of data availability is a problem. As we have argued above, the major adjustment problems communities face are likely to be in the immediate aftermath of the base closing. Thus, effective intervention to mitigate base closure effects requires timely information on those effects. However, the most systematic source of data on smaller communities is likely to be the U.S. census, which is administered only once each decade.

Although these data problems can be daunting, they are not insurmountable. Indeed, one of the most valuable contributions of this study may be its ability to demonstrate that short-term monitoring of community-level effects is possible. The study also suggests that, given the complexity of the closure process, it seems prudent for the Department of Defense, as well as state and local government, to collect data for existing bases and local communities. The purpose of this data collection is not only to predict the effects of future base closure on the communities that depend upon them but also to monitor those effects as they occur.

Appendix A
# SOURCES OF FORECASTS

As described in Chapter Four, economic impact analyses were prepared for each base scheduled for closure. These studies provided background information on the bases (employment levels, retiree populations, etc.) as well as the forecasts to which we compared the actual outcomes. For each of the bases, this appendix lists the studies consulted and the sources for each of the projected values cited.

## GEORGE AFB

The population projection is based on a forecast by Economics Research Associates (ERA), prepared for the marketing committee of the Victor Valley Economic Development Authority (Economic Research Associates, 1991a, Table III-4, p. III-4). The Victor Valley Union High School District (VVUHSD) enrollment projection is based on the expectation of the superintendent of the Victor Valley Union High School District; this was cited in Department of the Air Force (1991, p. 3-46). The employment projection, which is for Victor Valley, is based on Figure 3.4-2 in Department of the Air Force (1991, p. 3-28). The conversion to a percentage is approximate because it is based on a chart rather than on actual figures.

## CASTLE AFB

The Atwater Elementary enrollment projection is based on a forecast made by the Atwater Elementary School District; this was cited in California Military Base Reuse Task Force (1994, p. 11). The Merced County unemployment rate projection comes from page 9 of the same report. The population projection is based on forecasts by the Department of the Air Force (1994, Table 3.3-4).

## FORT ORD

The Monterey Peninsula Unified School District (MPUSD) enrollment projection is cited in a California Military Base Reuse Task Force (CMBRTF) report (1994, p. 11). The unemployment rate and retail sales projections are based on the worst-case forecast by a Congressional Budget Office (CBO) study (1992). The population and city revenue projections are based on figures in a report prepared for County of Monterey Administrative Office of Inter-Governmental Affairs, Salinas, California (RKG Associates, Inc., 1992, p. 14).

# Appendix B
# DATA SOURCES

## CITY DATA

The following figures (for all cities and years) are based on data provided by the California Department of Finance Demographic Research Unit: population, housing units, and vacancy rates.

The following figures (for all cities and years) are based on data provided by the Department of Labor Bureau of Labor Statistics, Local Area Unemployment Statistics Division: unemployment and labor force.

Municipal revenues figures are for total city revenues excluding debt. Source for all cities and years is the Office of the State Controller, Division of Local Government Fiscal Affairs, Bureau of Financial Reporting, City Unit.

K–12 enrollment figures are based on the number of students in each district who took the California Basic Education Data System test in October. Sources are the California Department of Education and local school districts.

Taxable retail sales figures are based on data provided by the California Board of Equalization Research and Statistics Division.

Housing prices for zip codes are quarterly figures based on median single-family residence prices. The source for all zip codes and years is Dataquick Information Systems; county home prices are based on data provided by the California Association of Realtors Research and Economics division.

Utilization figures for the County Hospital of Monterey Peninsula were provided by the County Hospital of Monterey Peninsula's accounting office.

Utilization figures for the Merced Community Medical Center were provided by the Merced Community Medical Center's chief financial officer; utilization figures for the Fremont/Rideout Health Group were provided by the Fremont/Rideout Health Group; utilization figures for Victor Valley Community Hospital were provided by the hospital's Human Resources and Community Services office.

## GEORGE AFB

Number of military personnel from FY 1987 through FY 1990 are based on George AFB Economic Resources Impact Statement Fiscal Years 1987, 1988, 1989, and 1990, cited in Economic Research Associates (1991b, Table 5). FY 1991 is from George AFB (1991, p. 7). Data from FY 1992 and FY 1993 are from the Department of Defense Manpower Data Center.

Percentage of military personnel living on- and off-base for FY 1987 through FY 1990 is based on George AFB Economic Resources Impact Statement Fiscal Years 1987, 1988, 1989 and 1990, cited in Economic Research Associates (1991b, Table 5). Data for FY 1991 are based on George AFB (1991, p. 7).

Data on military retirees in the area for FY 1987 through 1990 are based on Economic Research Associates (1991b, Table 5). For FY 1991, data are based on George AFB (1991, p. 7). Note that retirees in George AFB Economic Impact Region are represented by the following zip codes: 92301, 92307, 92342, 92345, 92368, 92371, 92372, 92394, and 92397.

Civilian personnel figures include appropriated fund civilians, nonappropriated funds, contract civilian, and private business. FY 1987 through FY 1990 are based on George AFB Economic Resources Impact Statement Fiscal Years 1987, 1988, 1989, and 1990, cited in Economic Research Associates (1991b, Table 5). FY 1991 is based on George AFB (1991, p. 7). FY 1992 and FY 1993 are based on Department of Defense Manpower Data Center data.

## CASTLE AFB

Military personnel for FY 1987 through FY 1991 are based on Department of the Air Force (1994, Table 3.3-2, p. 3-13). FY 1992 is based on Castle AFB (1992, Table 7, p. 7-1). 1993–1995 is based on data provided by the Castle AFB Public Affairs Office. 1993 data are for FY 1993. 1994 data are for October 14, 1994. 1995 data are based on monthly projections made on October 14, 1994. (Note: Military personnel includes military trainees and cadets.)

Percentage of military personnel living on- and off-base for FY 1987 through FY 1991 is based on Department of the Air Force (1994, Table 3.3-2, p. 3-13). Data for FY 1992 are based on Castle AFB (1992, Table 7, p. 7-1).

Military retirees in the area for FY 1987 through FY 1991 are from Department of the Air Force (1994, Table 3.3-2, p. 3-13). FY 1992 is based on Castle AFB (1992, Table 7, p. 7-1).

Civilian personnel for FY 1987 through FY 1991 are based on Department of the Air Force (1994, Table 3.3-2, p. 3-13). Data for FY 1992 are from Castle AFB (1992, Table 7, p. 7-1). Data for FY 1993 were provided by Tech Sgt. Armon T. Gaddy, Jr., Castle AFB Public Affairs Office. (Note: With the exception of FY 1993, these figures include appropriated fund civilians, nonappropriated funds, contract civilian, and private business. For FY 1993, data are for appropriated fund civilians only. Nonappropriated funds and other civilians are excluded.)

Data on residential locations are based on Department of the Air Force (1994, Table 3.3-3, p. 3-14).

## VANDENBERG AFB

All FY 1991 data (military personnel data, percentage of military personnel living on- and off-base, military retirees in area, civilian personnel) are from Vandenberg AFB (1991). Data for FY 1993 were provided by Vandenberg AFB 30th Space Wing Public Affairs. (Note: Military personnel includes military trainees and cadets.) The local impact area includes Santa Barbara and San Luis Obispo counties zip codes 934xx and 931xx. The civilian personnel figures include

Residential locations data are based on Economic Research Associates (1991, Table 6). According to the ERA report, "Data shown include all personnel for which information was available." Less than 1 percent of the sample resided outside of San Bernardino and Riverside counties. Additional data on residential locations is available in Department of the Air Force (1991, Table 3.1-1, p. 3-2).

## FORT ORD

Military personnel data for FY 1984 through FY 1991 are based on data provided by the Fort Ord Directorate of Resource Management, cited in RKG Associates, Inc. (1992, p. 46). Data for FY 1992 through FY 1994 are based on data supplied by the Department of Defense Manpower Data Center.

Percentage of military personnel living on- and off-base is based on RKG Associates, Inc. (1992, pp. 7–8). In particular, the authors of the RKG report state, "Approximately 15% of the Fort Ord military live off-base, usually in private sector rental housing. . . . A few individuals (estimated by the Fort Ord housing office at less than 75) own homes in the area."

Military retirees in the area are based on RKG Associates, Inc. (1992, p. 15). "An estimated 16,351 retired military personnel and their dependents live in the greater Monterey area, including nearby Santa Cruz and San Benito counties. This information was obtained from a recent Army survey of where retirement checks are sent and sorted for local communities."

Civilian personnel for FY 1984 through FY 1991 are based on data provided by the Fort Ord Directorate of Resource Management, cited in RKG Associates, Inc. (1992, p. 46). FY 1992 through FY 1994 data were supplied by the Department of Defense Manpower Data Center.

Residential locations data are based on RKG Associates, Inc. (1992, Figure I-3, p. 8).

appropriated fund civilians, nonappropriated funds, and private business. The FY 1991 figures exclude 3,835 aerospace contractor employees but include contract civilians not elsewhere included.

## CAMP PENDLETON

All FY 1992 data (military personnel data, percentage of military personnel living on- and off-base, military retirees in area, civilian personnel) are from Camp Pendleton (1993). Data for FY 1993 are from Camp Pendleton (1994).

## BEALE AFB

All FY 1992 data (military personnel data, percentage of military personnel living on- and off-base, military retirees in area, civilian personnel) are from Beale AFB (1992). Data for FY 1993 are from Beale AFB (1993).

# Appendix C
## LOCAL IMPACT AREAS

For each base that was closed, the local impact area comprises the cities included as part of the local redevelopment agency, typically the cities located closest to the base. Most data used are at the city level, but data on housing prices and the retiree population are derived from zip-code–level information. (See Table C.1 for a list of all relevant cities and their respective zip codes.)

The George Air Force Base Reuse Task Force consists of representatives of Adelanto, Victorville, Apple Valley, and Hesperia. The Fort Ord Reuse Group consists of Monterey County and the cities of Marina, Seaside, Del Rey Oaks, Sand City, Monterey, and Salinas. We excluded Sand City because of its small size (population <200) and conducted analyses with and without Salinas because its connections with Ord are not as close as those of the other communities. The reuse organization for Castle Air Force Base is the Castle Joint Powers Authority, which comprises Merced County and the cities of Atwater and Merced. Housing analyses of Castle AFB include data on Winton, a nearby unincorporated community. Winton was not included in the local impact area not only because it is not on the Castle Joint Powers Authority, but also because scant data are available on unincorporated areas.

For matched pairs, the local impact area comprises the cities located closest to the base in question. As a rule of thumb, we included cities within ten miles of the base. For Vandenberg AFB, we included Lompoc; for Camp Pendleton, Oceanside and Carlsbad; and for Beale AFB, Marysville and Yuba City.

## Table C.1

## Local Impact Area Cities and Their Zip Codes

| Location | Zip Code |
|---|---|
| Adelanto | 92301 |
| Apple Valley | 92307 |
| Apple Valley | 92308 |
| Atwater | 95301 |
| Carlsbad | 92008 |
| Carlsbad | 92009 |
| Hesperia | 92345 |
| Lompoc | 93436 |
| Lompoc | 93437 |
| Marina | 93933 |
| Marysville | 95901 |
| Merced | 95340 |
| Merced | 95348 |
| Monterey | 93940 |
| Oceanside | 92054 |
| Oceanside | 92055 |
| Oceanside | 92056 |
| Oceanside | 92057 |
| Pacific Grove | 93950 |
| Salinas | 93901 |
| Salinas | 93905 |
| Salinas | 93906 |
| Salinas | 93907 |
| Salinas | 93908 |
| Salinas | 93962 |
| Seaside | 93955 |
| Victorville | 92392 |
| Victorville | 92394 |
| Winton | 95388 |
| Yuba City | 95991 |
| Yuba City | 95993 |

# REFERENCES

Beale Air Force Base, *Beale AFB Economic Resource Impact Statement, Fiscal Year 1992*, September 30, 1992.

———, *Beale AFB Economic Resource Impact Statement, Fiscal Year 1993*, September 30, 1993.

Bradshaw, Ted K., *Which Impact? The Local Impact of Base Closure Needs Closer Examination*, Berkeley: Institute of Urban Development, University of California at Berkeley, IURD Working Paper No. 602, December 1993.

California Military Base Reuse Task Force, *Report of the California Military Base Reuse Task Force to Governor Pete Wilson: A Strategic Response to Base Reuse Opportunities*, Sacramento, Calif.: Governor's Office of Planning and Research, January 1994.

Camp Pendleton [U.S. Marine Corps], *Economic Impact Summary: Camp Pendleton California*, Joint Public Affairs Office, 1993.

———, *Economic Impact Summary: Camp Pendleton California*, Joint Public Affairs Office, 1994.

Castle Air Force Base, *Castle AFB Economic Resource Impact Statement Fiscal Year 1992*, September 30, 1992.

Commission on State Finance, *Defense Spending in the 1990s: Impact on California*, Sacramento, Calif.: Commission on State Finance, Summer 1990.

Daicoff, Darwin, Marston M. McCluggage, Charles K. Warrinor, and Ronald R. Olson, *Economic Impact of Military Base Closings*, Washington D.C.: Arms Control and Disarmament Agency, ACDA/E90, 1970.

Dertouzos, James, and Michael Dardia, *Defense Spending, Aerospace, and the California Economy*, Santa Monica, Calif.: RAND, MR-179-RC, 1993.

Economic Research Associates, *Draft Report: George AFB Reuse Market Analysis and Strategy*, Los Angeles, No. 9966, January 8, 1991a.

Economic Research Associates, *George Air Force Base Closure Socioeconomic Impact Upon the City of Victorville*, Los Angeles, Ca., No. 10382, November 1991b.

George Air Force Base, *George AFB Economic Resource Impact Statement Fiscal Year 1991*, September 30, 1991.

Innes, Judith, Ted K. Bradshaw, Cynthia Kroll, Rokaya Al-Ayat, Mary Corley, Lyn Harlan, Josh Kirschenbaum, Jason Moody, *Defense Industry Conversion, Base Closure, and the California Economy*, Berkeley: Institute of Urban and Regional Development, Center for Real Estate and Urban Economics, University of California at Berkeley, November 1994.

Krop, Cathy R., Steven J. Carroll, and Randy L. Ross, *Tracking K–12 Education Spending in California*, Santa Monica, Calif.: RAND, MR-548-SFR, 1995.

MacKinnon, David A., "Military Base Closures: Long Range Effects and Implications for Industrial Development," *AID.C. Journal*, 13(3), July 1978, pp. 7–41.

Office of Economic Adjustment, *Civilian Reuse of Former Military Bases: A Summary of Completed Military Base Adjustment Projects*, Washington, D.C., U.S. Department of Defense, September 1993.

Pine, Art, "Pentagon to Seek Fewer Base Closings in 1995 Cutbacks," *Los Angeles Times*, January 27, 1995, p. A5.

Ricks, Thomas, "Latest Round of Military Base Closings by Pentagon Falls Short of Expectations," *Wall Street Journal*, March 1, 1995, p. A6.

RKG Associates, Inc., *Economic Impact Analysis of the Downsizing of Fort Ord on Monterey County*, Durham, N.H.: RKG Associates, Inc., June 1992.

Schmitt, Eric, "A Mission Accomplished," *New York Times*, June 29, 1993, p. A10.

U.S. Department of the Air Force, *Draft Socioeconomic Impact Analysis Study: Disposal and Reuse of George Air Force Base, California*, Washington, D.C.: Department of Defense, Alexandria, Va.: Defense Technical Information Center, September 1991.

U.S. Department of the Air Force, *Socioeconomic Impact Analysis Study: Disposal and Reuse of Castle Air Force Base, California*, Alexandria, Va.: Defense Technical Information Center, January 1994.

U.S. Department of Defense, *The Relationship between Base Closures/Realignments and Non-DoD Federal Costs*, Washington, D.C., September 1994.

Vandenberg Air Force Base, *Vandenberg AFB Economic Resource Impact Statement, Fiscal Year 1991*, September 30, 1991.